**FA**
**QUIZ**

# THE
# FAMILY
# QUIZ BOOK

### EDITED BY
### ELIZABETH YOUNG

BLANDFORD PRESS
POOLE · DORSET

First published
in this compilation in the U.K. 1984
by Blandford Press, Link House,
West Street, Poole, Dorset, BH15 1LL

Reprinted 1984

Copyright © Blandford Press Ltd

**British Library Cataloguing in Publication Data**

The Family quiz book.
  1. Questions and answers
  I. Young, Elizabeth
  793.73          AG195

    ISBN 0 7137 1454 9

Typeset by Inforum Ltd, Portsmouth
Printed in Great Britain
by Richard Clay (The Chaucer Press) Ltd, Bungay, Suffolk

# CONTENTS

# QUESTIONS

Who sold his birthright for a mess of potage?
What is an abbess?
What does a cooper manufacture?
Name the most famous writers of fairy stories.
What is a tourniquet?
From where does the following expression come:
'Grinning like a Cheshire cat'?
Where did Shakespeare live in his youth?
Name the female fox.
Give the date of Lady Day.
What is a coney?
What do you know of Mecca?
What is a teal?
Who founded Rome?
Who shot an arrow through an apple on his son's head?
How many humps has a dromedary?
Who is the Patron Saint of Wales?
What is a hall mark?
Give the meaning of 'fait accompli'.
In which year did Queen Elizabeth II ascend the throne?
With what was corn threshed prior to the threshing
machine?

1 What is a person who studies moths and butterflies called
2 What is a campanologist?
3 What were the contestants in a Roman arena called?
4 Where was Drake playing bowls when the Armada was reported?
5 What do we call a man who stuffs fishes and other animals?
6 What sport did Winston Churchill play as a young man?
7 What distinctive award was given to winners of races in th ancient Olympic Games?
8 What game was played in an extraordinary manner in *Alice in Wonderland*?
9 What ball game is a feature of *Tom Brown's Schooldays*?
10 What is toxophily?
11 Where is the 'Wall Game' played?
12 Which British Prime Minister owned a Derby winner?
13 What was the main event in a medieval tournament?
14 Which 16th century author refers to billiards?
15 What do the letters P.G.A. stand for?
16 Which Roman sport is a feature of *Ben Hur*?
17 Between which two towns was the first marathon run?
18 What is a 'clay pigeon'?
19 What are the 'Queensberry Rules'?
20 What kind of event is the Calgary Stampede?

What was the name of Esau's brother?
What is an Imam?
Who was the first king of Israel?
What is the meaning of the name Jesus?
In what faith is the goddess Durga worshipped?
In the Bible, where did the ark come to rest when the flood abated?
What did the dove bring back when it was sent out for the second time from the ark?
What is Eid ul Fitr?
In the Christian religion who is the patron saint of animals?
Who made Christianity the official religion of the Roman Empire?
In the Bible on what were the Commandments written?
What is the title of the Bishop of Rome?
What does a Jew understand by 'teraifa'?
In the Old Testament who fashioned the golden calf?
Who was the Roman god of fire?
Which Christian saint died a martyr's death on a spiked wheel?
What is the principal book of the Islamic faith?
Where did Sikhism begin?
What is the name for the Jewish place of worship?
Where did Muhammad die?

1 What is a howdah?
2 Who founded the Sunday Schools?
3 What is homicide?
4 What distinguishes a Manx cat?
5 What is a hiatus?
6 Give the name for a young swan.
7 What is a metronome?
8 What is a hyperbole?
9 What do the initials B.B.C. stand for?
10 What and when is Candlemas?
11 Who was the founder of the Jesuits?
12 Where does the following quotation appear: 'Friends, Romans, Countrymen, lend me your ears'?
13 What do you understand by 'quarto'?
14 Who are the Zulus?
15 What is the meaning of 'ex officio'?
16 What is the White House?
17 Name the industry for which Amsterdam is famous.
18 How many sheets of paper are there to a quire?
19 What is the meaning of intestate?
20 What is a cliché?

1 Linen is made from what plant?
2 What is jarrah?
3 What is cellulose?
4 What is a peduncle?
5 Where do we get raffia from?
6 Which tree, according to legend, was once a Greek nymph?
7 What is the oldest tree of our planet?
8 What is the name given to the green colouring matter in plants?
9 To which family do the following belong: maize, wheat, sugar-cane, rice, barley and bamboo?
10 Where do we obtain turpentine from?
11 What is a perennial plant?
12 What is the name given to rubber as it flows from a tapped tree?
13 From what is rice paper obtained?
14 Which two spices come from the same Java tree?
15 With which flower do we associate Australia?
16 What is the cambium layer, and what does it do?
17 Which is the odd one out, and why: Japanese oak, redwood, birch and ash?
18 Laudanum is an anaesthetic. From where is it obtained?
19 What is cork?
20 The oil from certain Australian trees can be used as an antiseptic. What are the trees?

1 Give the three names we often use to express ordinary men.
2 What is the title of Jerome K. Jerome's best-known book
3 Give the names of the three men in the fiery furnace.
4 Who sailed off in a wooden shoe?
5 Where did the three Kings of Orient go?
6 What Biblical character was visited by three 'comforters
7 Give the title of a famous nursery round in which three animals are the subject.
8 Give the title of a nursery rhyme in which three fiddlers appear.
9 Who lost their mittens?
10 In which of Shakespeare's plays do three witches appear
11 What is a hat with three points called?
12 What is it that three people are not?
13 What are three musical performers called?
14 What is an object which has three prongs?
15 What is a three-legged stand for holding a kettle?
16 Who wrote *The Three Musketeers*?
17 Where do Three Little Maids from School appear?
18 Who are the three sisters who wrote under pen names?
19 What are three monkeys often depicted as warning us no to do?
20 An heraldic bearing, representing three lilies (the royal arms of France).

1 What was Excalibur?
2 Who created the character Don Quixote?
3 Give the origin of the Pentecost.
4 What is braille?
5 Name the male of goose.
6 What is an ailurophobe?
7 Give the date of Michaelmas.
8 What are the territorial divisions of France called?
9 What is a cachalot?
0 What does the musical term 'fortissimo' mean?
1 When is Holy Week?
2 What is gutta percha?
3 Who was Marconi?
4 Name the only metal which is liquid at ordinary
   temperatures.
5 For what does 'D' stand in Roman figures?
6 What is the diameter of the Earth?
7 What is a centimetre?
8 What was the Feudal system?
9 What is an ingot?
0 Which part of the church is the nave?

1 A fool and what are soon parted?
2 All that glitters is not . . . . .?
3 The saying points out that there is no need to take them
  Newcastle.
4 All these lead to Rome, so the saying tells us.
5 As right as a trivet means what?
6 Under certain circumstances they should never be throw
7 Sticks and stones may break my bones, but . . . . . will
  never hurt me.
8 What never boils?
9 In for a . . . . . in for a pound.
10 Fair play is a . . . . .
11 Kind hearts are more than . . . . .
12 Which is mightier than what?
13 Wordsworth said to Milton, 'Thy soul was like a . . . . .
14 Where the camel will not go.
15 Why did Midas live to regret the granting of his dearest
  wish?
16 According to the saying, when should one strike?
17 'Stone walls do not a prison make, nor . . . . . a cage.'
18 What, according to the saying, is an Englishman's home
19 What did John of Gaunt (in Shakespeare's *Richard the
  Second*) describe as a precious stone?
20 Who said, 'What, only 20 talents? I will give you 50 tale
  for my life'?

Who was the first Australian to win the men's singles championship of the United States?

What is the length of a tennis court?

How did the Davis Cup originate?

How often is the Davis Cup competed for?

Who won the Wimbledon men's singles title in 1983?

Who won the Wimbledon ladies' singles title in 1983?

In which year did Virginia Wade win the Wimbledon ladies' singles title?

How many points are required to win a standard tie-break?

Under what circumstances is a double hit allowed?

Which player serves in the first game after a tie-break?

What was Evonne Cawley's maiden name?

Who won the Wimbledon men's singles title in 1973, the year that the tournament was boycotted by the Association of Tennis Professionals?

Who won the Wightman Cup in 1983?

Which record did Elizabeth Ryan hold until one day after her death?

Which are the Grand Slam tournaments?

Who won the men's singles at the French Open in 1983?

Where is the U.S. Open now held?

Who was generally acclaimed as 'the best player never to win Wimbledon'?

Who is the only man ever to have won five singles titles in a row at Wimbledon?

Which South African doubles specialist was famous for his white cap?

1 Who wrote *Jane Eyre*?
2 What is dermatitis?
3 To whom was the name 'the Beloved Physician' applied
4 Give the meaning of 'persona grata'.
5 What dangerous gas is given off when coke is burned?
6 What is a hygrometer?
7 What and where is the Kremlin?
8 What is an abattoir?
9 Who takes the title of Excellency?
10 What is the size of a Crown sheet of paper?
11 To whom was the name the Swedish Nightingale applie
12 Who used the nom de plume Mark Twain?
13 What is a man-hour?
14 Who wrote *The Deserted Village*?
15 What is an emulsion?
16 How many lines are there in a sonnet?
17 Who was President of U.S.A. during the First World W
18 Who wrote and composed *The Pirates of Penzance*?
19 For what was the Schneider Trophy awarded?
20 What is endive?

What is meant by a debut album?

What are Billboard and Cashbox?

What do the abbreviations NME and MM mean to a British pop fan?

British TV has the world's longest running weekly pop music show. What is it called?

Dick Clark was host on a long running teenage pop music show in the USA. What was it called?

Who was Allan Freed?

Who or what is ELO?

Hit Parade, the Charts, Hot 100 and Top 20 are all names for what?

What is a synthesizer?

Which piano playing rock'n'roller is associated with *Great Balls of Fire*?

Which famous group had only a modest success with their first record *Love Me Do*?

Which famous group's first record was entitled *Come On*?

Which American rock'n'roll singers died in a plane crash in February 1959?

Which American rock'n'roll singer died after a car crash in England in April 1960?

Who or what is or was ABBA?

Which famous record label and pop music style was named after the American city of Detroit?

What is a Number 1?

Discs, platters, sides, 45s are all popular names for what?

The world's only nationwide pop music radio station commenced in 1967. What is it called?

What are Bluebeat, Ska, Rocksteady and Reggae?

1 What is the capital of Tasmania?
2 Which city is often known as Auld Reekie?
3 Who, or what was, 'Mistress of the Adriatic'?
4 Which city stands on the Moskva River?
5 Name the capital of Switzerland.
6 Which well known Russian City was built partly on rub
brought from London after the Great Fire?
7 Islamabad is capital of what country?
8 Which city in America is the holy city of the Mormon s
9 What is the capital of the Malagasy Republic?
10 What is the name of the capital of Brazil?
11 What do you know of Constantinople, Byzantium and
Istanbul?
12 Why is Southampton a remarkable and useful port?
13 Where would you be if you were in Addis Ababa? Wha
the country's other name?
14 Where did the Pilgrim Fathers land? What year was it?
15 What was the ancient name for the city of Rome?
16 In which cities would you find: Champs Elysees, Princ
Street, Broadway and Regent Street?
17 Which is the odd one out, and why: London, Cardiff,
Birmingham, Edinburgh, Belfast?
18 What have the following in common: Kairhouan, Mec
Rome, Kandy?
19 What have the following cities in common, and where a
they: Pittsburg, Sheffield?
20 Which town, not the capital, is the busiest in the count
is built on some two hundred islands, and is noted for i
diamond trade and zoological gardens?

1. What does the term 'circa' mean?
2. Where is the mezzanine floor?
3. Who spoke these words 'Dr Livingstone, I presume'? What was his profession?
4. What is truffle?
5. What is the colour of a starboard light on a ship?
6. What is rickets?
7. Who was George Romney?
8. What is probate?
9. How many sides has a hexagon?
10. What is the sex of a glow-worm?
11. Who was Chippendale?
12. For what is Kimberley noted?
13. Where is this quotation to be found: 'He that hath ears to hear let him hear'?
14. What is a tyro?
15. What is a Bourse?
16. What does the term Upper Ten mean?
17. The height of a horse is reckoned in hands: what is a hand?
18. What is the National Trust?
19. Which side of a ship is called starboard?
20. Will the year 2000 be a leap-year?

1 Who wrote under the nom-de-plume 'Boz'?
2 Who wrote *Coriolanus*?
3 In which book does the character Sam Weller appear?
4 In which book does the character Becky Sharp appear?
5 What is Hans Christian Andersen famous for?
6 Who wrote *Little Women*?
7 Which novelist became Governor-General of Canada?
8 Who created the character of Peter Pan?
9 Who created the character of Christopher Robin?
10 On what serious subject did the author of *Alice in Wonderland* write?
11 Who originated the following detectives?
   (a) Sherlock Holmes
   (b) Father Brown
12 Who wrote *The Good Companions*?
13 Who is the Father of English literature?
14 Name the famous novelist sisters who lived at Haworth
15 Who is the author of *Cranford*?
16 What was the nationality of Mark Twain?
17 Who was Dr. Johnson's biographer?
18 What man in a story by Washington Irving experienced a very long sleep?
19 Which famous English poet died at Missolonghi?
20 Who conceived the fictitious country of Lilliput?

What is meant by allergy?
What is amnesia?
What is analgesia?
In connection with which disease is insulin used?
What is an antidote?
Give the common term for arteriosclerosis?
To what part of the body does astigmatism apply?
What causes beri-beri?
Give the popular term for botulism.
Which foods come under the heading carbohydrates?
Which part of the body does cataract affect?
What is the symptom of claustrophobia?
What do we call enlargement of the thyroid gland?
How is hydrophobia brought about?
What is the term for a person who always imagines he is ill?
What do you understand by pancreas?
Where is the pituitary gland situated?
What is another name for trachea?
Give a more usual name for vertigo.
Where does a whitlow form?

1 What does 'ibid' mean?
2 At what temperature Centigrade does water freeze?
3 What is a kris?
4 Who was Michael Faraday?
5 Who were the Magi?
6 What is Thomas Gainsborough famed for?
7 What is an inventory?
8 What did John Evelyn and Samuel Pepys have in common?
9 Who first flew the Atlantic?
10 What is produced in Gruyère?
11 Give the meaning of 'sine qua non'.
12 What is an incumbent?
13 What is the sign of a pawnbroker?
14 Who wrote *Paradise Lost*?
15 Where is Tomsk?
16 Who was Lenin?
17 What is meant by 'coup de grâce'?
18 When is Innocents Day?
19 What is the boiling point of water in degrees Fahrenhei
20 What is an obelisk?

Where is the world-famous church of St. Mark?

Where is the Leaning Tower?

What is the name of the Cathedral of Paris?

What is the highest structure in Paris?

What is erected off the entrance to New York Harbour?

What are the famous landmarks at Giza?

Name the most famous group of buildings in Moscow.

Name an ancient Druid temple in Wiltshire, England.

What bridge in Scotland is outstanding in structure and engineering?

What is the famous cemetery in Washington, D.C.?

Name the famous mountain at Cape Town.

What famous rock guards the entrance to the Mediterranean?

Name a bridge which spans a deep gorge at Bristol.

Name a famous volcano on Sicily.

What is the highest point in the world?

What is the most westerly point of England?

Where is the Bridge of Sighs?

Where is the Parthenon?

Where is the Alhambra?

Where is the Pompidou Centre?

1 In which year did the yacht race for the America's Cup originate?
2 With which sport do you associate the name of Larry Holmes?
3 Who was the 1983 world motor racing champion?
4 What is an épee?
5 In which sport is a 'puck' used?
6 Which American was world speedway Champion in 1981 and 1982?
7 Name the Australian brothers who made their names in international golf and test cricket respectively in the 1970s?
8 In which game is a shuttlecock used?
9 With which game do you associate the Jets, the Raiders and the Cowboys?
10 Who won the men's singles at Wimbledon in 1982?
11 Who won the 1982 World Cup in Football?
12 With which sport do you associate the name of Ian Botham?
13 Which famous Danish speedway rider retired in 1983?
14 Which international rugby team are called the 'All Blacks'?
15 In American football, how many points are scored for a touchdown?
16 Which yacht race starts from the Isle of Wight and finishes in Plymouth, going via S.W. Ireland?
17 Which sport is associated with the name of Jehengir Khan?
18 Where and when were the first world championships in athletics held?
19 What unusual feat did Carl Lewis perform at these championships?
20 Who achieved a record score for free dance in the 1983 world ice-dancing championships?

What is the *Flying Dutchman*?

What is copra?

Who was John Dryden?

What is an anodyne?

What is the Parliament or legislative assembly of Norway called?

What is the Plimsoll Line?

What are spoonerisms?

Name the two most important canals in the world.

What was the *Mayflower*?

Which book is the world's best seller?

What is a 'Blue Peter'?

Where is the famous thoroughfare Unter den Linden?

What is a minuet?

What is 'felo de se'?

Which Scottish loch is reputed to be inhabited by a monster?

What is an albino?

Who was William Wilberforce?

What is the meaning of 'a Roland for an Oliver'?

What distinction does Malta hold?

Who were the suffragettes?

1 What is a dingo?
2 What is the name given to the wild or half-tamed horse California?
3 What are the colours of a skewbald?
4 Which is the fastest animal?
5 How fast can a racehorse gallop over short distances?
6 What is a prairie dog?
7 What is (a) a colt, (b) an onager?
8 Which cats have tufted ears?
9 Who, or what, was the nursemaid to the Darling childn in Peter Pan?
10 What is a jennet?
11 What is a panther?
12 What is the common name for *Canis lupus*?
13 What type of animal takes its name from Przewalski?
14 What is a breeding female of a domestic cat known as?
15 Who went with the three men in a boat?
16 What is an ounce?
17 What word means 'cat-like'?
18 Which animal's Latin name means 'cat-footed'?
19 What is the common name for the Arabian gazelle hou
20 In what continent is the jaguar naturally found?

1. How many lions are there on the British Royal Standard?
2. On which flag would you find a giraffe?
3. On the arms of Norway what animal holds an axe?
4. Which coat-of-arms is supported by an emu and a kangaroo?
5. Which country had the Lion of Judah emblazoned in the middle of its flag?
6. On which arms will you find a dove with an olive branch in its beak?
7. What animal can be seen on the flag of Berlin?
8. A vehicle displaying the international identity mark CH would be from which country?
9. Which creature symbolises France?
10. Which creatures are seen on the flags of the following: Gambia; Virgin Islands?
11. What animal is shown on the flag of California?
12. Which countries do you associate with the beaver, kiwi and dragon?
13. What ships fly the red ensign?
14. Where would you find an eagle with a snake in its mouth?
15. What two implements appear on the flag of the USSR?
16. From which country would an aircraft be if it displayed N as its international registration mark?
17. Where can you see a yellow star above a two-headed eagle, all on a red background?
18. Which flags are incorporated in the Union Jack?
19. Which animal is found on the badge of the Knight Templars?
20. The flag of which country consists of red, yellow and black vertical stripes?

1 What is associated with Pearl Harbor?
2 On what river does Bonn stand?
3 Who was Nebuchadnezzar?
4 What was the maiden name of Shakespeare's wife?
5 What is par?
6 Give the meaning of 'volte-face'.
7 Who wrote the play *Pygmalion*?
8 Which Irish river's water possesses special qualities for brewing?
9 What is an agate?
10 Who was Calvin?
11 What is the chief material used in making glass?
12 Which was the German battleship which scuttled itself off Montevideo?
13 What was the Black Death?
14 When is Quinquagesima?
15 What is a coalition?
16 Which composer became stone deaf?
17 What is a caret?
18 What is a Khaki Campbell?
19 Who was known as The Immortal Bard?
20 Who was William Willett?

*Who created the following characters:*

1 Lemuel Gulliver
2 Captain Hornblower
3 Dr. Dolittle
4 Scarlett O'Hara
5 Professor Higgins
6 Soames Forsyte
7 Sir Roger de Coverley
8 Apollyon
9 Heathcliff
10 Baron Frankenstein
11 Mrs. Malaprop
12 Rogue Herries
13 Huckleberry Finn
14 Sairey Gamp
15 Becky Sharp
16 Christopher Robin
17 Marguerite Gauthier
18 Richard Hannay
19 Jo March
20 Starveling the Tailor

1 For how long may a player search for a ball before it is deemed lost?
2 What is the length of a standard driver?
3 How frequently does the Ryder Cup take place?
4 What is the diameter of the hole?
5 May a match be discontinued because of bad weather?
6 Which Australian player won the World Matchplay Championships in 1983?
7 Which golfer's nickname is 'The Bear'?
8 Name Germany's best golfer since the war?
9 What does the term 'eagle' denote?
10 In matchplay, what does 'Dormy 2' mean?
11 In which year did European players join the British Ryder Cup team?
12 Where was the British Open held in its first eleven years?
13 Where is the U.S. Masters always played?
14 What is the maximum number of clubs permitted during a round of golf?
15 Where is the headquarters of the Royal & Ancient Club, commonly known as the 'home of golf'?
16 Who won the U.S. Masters in 1983?
17 Who is known as 'The Walrus'?
18 What is a 'scratch' golfer?
19 Which iron club was previously known as a 'mashie'?
20 Who competes for the Walker Cup?

What are Sikhs?
What is a 'concierge'?
What is a misanthrope?
What is connected with St. Moritz?
Who was Paul Jones?
'E. and O.E.' often appears on invoices and accounts.
What is the meaning?
What does R.V. stand for?
What is a gargoyle?
What is a verst?
How long is the Great Wall of China?
What is a lunar month?
Who was Confucius?
What is a spa?
When it is 12 noon in London what time is it in New York?
Name the keyboards on a four-manual organ.
What is a hydrometer?
Who was Van Dyke?
Describe a vignette.
What is a crustacean?
Give the name of the Negro who was the world's
champion heavy weight boxer during the early part of this
century.

*Provide the completing half of the following phrases:*

1 Stocks and —
2 Part and —
3 Spick and —
4 Pestle and —
5 Pots and —
6 Tooth and —
7 Brimstone and —
8 Safe and —
9 Brace and —
10 Darby and —
11 Ball and —
12 Frills and —
13 Goods and —
14 Bag and —
15 Hole and —
16 Rack and —
17 Sackcloth and —
18 Hue and —
19 Ways and —
20 Birds and —

Name the capital of Finland.
Where are the Straits of Magellan?
To what country does Alaska belong?
Is Antrim in Northern Ireland or Eire?
What is the name of the sandbanks off Deal?
What does the Menai Bridge connect with the mainland?
What is the highest mountain in Great Britain?
Name the famous bay on the west coast of France.
Where is Madagascar? What is its other name?
Where is Timbuctoo?
Where is Tipperary?
Is Burma to the east or west of India?
Where is the Gobi Desert?
What two seas does the Bosphorus join?
On what lake is Toronto situated?
In which Australian State is Melbourne?
Where are the Iguassu falls?
Where is the Yosemite Valley?
Which two seas does the Suez Canal join?
Between which two countries does the Simplon Tunnel run?

1 Describe a cornucopia.
2 Which town in the U.S.A. is known as the 'windy city'
3 What is an adze?
4 Who was Minerva?
5 What is the Te Deum?
6 Give the plural of talisman.
7 What is a bi-centenary?
8 What was the name of Ahab's wife?
9 What is linseed?
10 Who composed *The Blue Danube*?
11 Who was Sir Truby King?
12 What do printers call (i) capital letters and (ii) small letters?
13 What is a loofah?
14 What was the Witanagemot?
15 From what is saccharin derived?
16 What is astigmatism?
17 What are the hours of a 'dog-watch'?
18 What is the science of numismatics?
19 What do the letters Ph.D stand for?
20 What is an articled pupil?

1 What is the official home of the Lord Mayor of London?
2 Where is the most famous Woolworth Building?
3 Where are Silbury Hill and Stonehenge?
4 What famous royal castle is in Berkshire?
5 What famous statue stands on Bedloe's Island?
6 Which is 'the other place', mentioned by Members of the House of Commons?
7 Where would you find the Piazza San Pietro?
8 Where were the Hanging Gardens? Who built them?
9 Which country first landed a rocket on the moon?
10 What stone buildings stand between Giza and Memphis?
11 Which is the largest of these buildings?
12 What was the name of the huge lighthouse built on an island off the North African coast?
13 Off what coast was the greatest pre-fabricated harbour anchored?
14 What is the Pantheon? What was it used for?
15 What is the name of the sacred building at Mecca which holds the black stone?
16 Where would you find two churches, one above the other, and round the walls of the upper church painted scenes from the life of a saint?
17 Where was the Tower of Babel?
18 Where was the Colossus?
19 What is the connection between Heliopolis, New York and London?
20 Where is the Alhambra? What is it?

1 What early English book did what author write in priso
2 What famous poem was written about, and in, prison, a by whom?
3 What school did Tom Brown attend?
4 Who went to Buckingham Palace with Christopher Rol
5 What cities did what author write about in *A Tale of Tw Cities*?
6 What were the names of Louisa M. Alcott's Little Women?
7 Charles Lamb wrote '*The Essays of . . .*'?
8 What were the three imaginary countries visited by Lemuel Gulliver?
9 Who created Utopia?
10 Who created Erewhon?
11 Where did Lord Byron die?
12 Of whom and by whom was it said, 'He was not of an a but for all time!'?
13 Of whom and by whom was it said that he was 'inebriat with the exuberance of his own verbosity'?
14 Of whom and by whom was it said, 'I loved the man, ar do honour his memory, on this side idolatory, as much any'?
15 Who wrote: 'When I am dead, I hope it may be said: "I sins were scarlet, but his books were read" '?
16 What was the name of the dog in *Three Men in a Boat*?
17 Who disguised herself as a Doctor of Laws?
18 Who escaped from prison disguised as a washerwoman
19 What name did Shakespeare's heroine Julia assume wh masquerading as a man?
20 Who assumed numerous disguises in order to rescue aristocrats from the guillotine during the French Revolution?

To whom was the name 'The Iron Duke' applied?
What two diverse things do you associate with Covent Garden?
Who was Simon Bolivar?
Name the female of the drake.
For what number does MDCCCLXVI stand?
What is the Salic Law?
What is a chameleon?
Who is said to have fiddled while Rome burned?
Give the meaning of 'faux pas'.
Who was the Maid of Orleans?
What is a halibut?
Where and what are The Needles?
Who is the author of Vanity Fair?
What is a 'jack of all trades'?
Where is Emmanuel College?
What is cribbage?
In which town did Lady Godiva ride?
Who was the author of the Scarlet Pimpernel books?
What is a yak?
What is a yam?

*Give the meaning of the following:*

1 Ad infinitum
2 Ad valorem
3 A la mode
4 A propos
5 Au fait
6 Bête noire
7 Bona fide
8 Comme il faut
9 Coup d'état
10 Coup de grace
11 De trop
12 En masse
13 En route
14 Entre nous
15 Erratum
16 Hors de combat
17 Laissez faire
18 Sub judice
19 Vis-à-vis
20 Quo vadis?

1 What is an escalop?
2 Which spirit is usually drunk with haggis?
3 What is Russia's national drink?
4 What is a 'hot dog'?
5 What is the difference between 'à la carte' and 'table d'hôte'?
6 From what animal do we get veal?
7 From what is Roquefort cheese made?
8 What are clams?
9 What are canapes?
10 What is endive?
11 What is paté de fois gras?
12 What is the correct way of eating asparagus?
13 Whose nests are used for bird's nest soup?
14 What is an aperitif?
15 What is a calorie?
16 What is the name for body-building foods?
17 What insurance institution started in a coffee house?
18 What are the two main ingredients of a bloody Mary?
19 Which is the higher in calories, the yolk or the white of an egg?
20 With what would you expect a dish to be flavoured if it is described as 'provençal'?

1 In what book does Tiny Tim appear?
2 What river flows through Oxford?
3 Of what does air consist?
4 What is a steeplejack?
5 What is a 'crow's nest'?
6 What is litmus paper?
7 For what number does XLII stand?
8 Give the colours of the rainbow.
9 What is a mulatto?
10 Who was the boy who has the reputation of never having told a lie?
11 Who composed the *1812 Overture*?
12 Who was found in the bulrushes by Pharaoh's daughter?
13 What gifts did the Three Wise Men bring to the Infant Jesus?
14 On what island was St. Paul shipwrecked?
15 What are the three secondary colours?
16 What is the meaning of 'post meridian'?
17 Which nation first used tanks as weapons of war?
18 What is a stalactite?
19 What is an ampersand?
20 Who was the author of *Mein Kampf*?

1 Who was the wife of Napoleon?
2 Who married William of Orange?
3 What was the name of the Duchess of Windsor before her
  marriage to the Duke?
4 Who did Robert Browning marry?
5 Who was the first husband of Mary, Queen of Scots?
6 Who was the wife of Louis XVI?
7 Who was the bride of William Shakespeare?
8 Who did Ruth marry?
9 Who were Jacob's two wives?
0 Who was Henry VIII's first wife?
1 Who was Queen Victoria's consort?
2 Who was the first Red Indian bride of an Englishman?
3 Who did Emma Woodhouse marry?
4 Who was the wife of Othello?
5 Who was the husband of Guinevere?
6 Whose wife looked back?
7 Whose wife was the most famous authority on cookery?
8 What man and wife are associated with Dotheboy's Hall?
9 Who wrote: 'A good hanging prevents a bad marriage'?
0 What was Diana the Princess of Wales' maiden name?

*Complete the following pairs:*

1 Gilbert and —
2 *Lion and* —
3 *The Walrus and* —
4 Hengist and —
5 Anthony and —
6 Ancient and —
7 Romulus and —
8 Sodom and —
9 Gog and —
10 *Dombey and* —
11 Venus and —
12 Samson and —
13 Tweedledum and —
14 Hansel and —
15 Medes and —
16 William and —
17 Laurel and —
18 Rodgers and —
19 Ginger Rogers and —
20 Starsky and —

Whose daughter was Cassandra?
What are the territorial divisions of Switzerland called?
What is the Vatican?
What is a cable's length?
What is a tonsure?
Does hot air rise or fall?
What is a clerk in Holy Orders?
Which came first, Psalms or Proverbs in the order of the Bible?
What was the name of the little boy who never grew up, and who was his creator?
What is an oast house?
Why are policemen sometimes called 'bobbies'?
What is papyrus?
Who composed *Moonlight Sonata*?
What was Thailand previously named?
What does 'Ich Dien' mean and whose motto is it?
Who was the first woman to fly from Great Britain to Australia?
What was the former name of Istanbul?
What is 22 carat gold?
How many legs has a fly?
Who produced the first English Dictionary?

*Who wrote:*

1 *Whiteoaks*
2 *Laburnum Grove*
3 *The Holly and the Ivy*
4 *Under the Greenwood Tree*
5 *The Corn is Green*
6 *The Flower of May*
7 *The Trembling of a Leaf*
8 *The Grapes of Wrath*
9 *The Cherry Orchard*
10 *The Flowering Cherry*
11 *The Wind in the Willows*
12 *Magnolia Street*
13 *Flowers for Mrs. Harris*
14 *The Apple Cart*
15 *The Green Bay Tree*
16 *The Nutmeg Tree*
17 *The Darling Buds of May*
18 *Mary Rose*
19 *Green Apple Harvest*
20 *The Black Tulip*

*What are the missing words, and from which author do these quotations come?*

Sail on, O . . . of State
Out, damn'd . . . , out, I say
Neither cast ye your pearls before . . .
Heap . . . of fire upon his head
Hail to thee, blithe spirit!    thou never wert
The . . .'s lot is not a happy one
To . . . is human, to forgive divine
A . . . of beauty is a joy for ever
The world is too much with us; late and soon
Getting and spending, we lay waste our . . .
Where ignorance is bliss
'Tis . . . to be wise
I shot an . . . into the air
Jacob saw there was . . . in Egypt
Of shoes and ships and . . .
Of cabbages and kings
Our little . . . have their day,
They have their day and cease to be
He also serves who only . . . and waits
The . . . and the shouting dies,
The captains and the kings depart
My kingdom for a . . .
The race is not to the . . .
A . . . may look at a king
The quality of . . . is not strained

1 Name the seed of the oak tree.
2 What is an Eisteddfod?
3 From what does liquorice come?
4 What is a spinster?
5 What is rubber?
6 What is the normal temperature of the human body?
7 Give the year of the Battle of Waterloo.
8 What is a lemming?
9 How long is a metre in terms of inches?
10 Which is the highest rank in the Royal Air Force?
11 What is the signature of the Archbishop of Canterbury
12 Give the meaning of 'quid pro quo'.
13 Who wrote *Rhapsody in Blue*?
14 Where is Table Mountain?
15 What does U.S.S.R. stand for?
16 To what family does the ladybird belong?
17 What do you understand by a 'man of straw?'
18 What is a greenhorn?
19 Whose statue stands in Trafalgar Square?
20 What is nectar?

1 Name a grinning cat.
2 What was the name of the white wolf hound?
3 What was the name of Rudyard Kipling's mongoose?
4 In what poem does Samuel Taylor Coleridge refer to an albatross?
5 Name the great white whale.
6 Who was the donkey who went on a journey through France?
7 In which work did a walrus walk with a carpenter?
8 Who went to sea in a 'beautiful pea-green boat'?
9 What was a 'wee, sleekit cow'rin' tim'rous beastie'?
10 What was the name of the cat drowned in a tub of gold-fishes?
11 Who was the large dog acting as nursemaid to a family of three children?
12 What was the name of Anna Sewell's mare?
13 Who was the rabbit who lived with a squirrel and a hare?
14 Who carried a large pocket-watch and kept saying 'Oh, my ears and whiskers, I will be late!'?
15 Who wrote about a boastful toad?
16 What animal was put into a pot of tea?
17 Who had a parrot called Captain Flint?
18 Who wrote of a thieving jackdaw?
19 In what poem were rats the villains?
20 On what animal was the following written by Caroline Norton:
'My beautiful, my beautiful, that standest meekly by,
    With thy proudly arched and glossy neck, and dark
            and fiery eye.'?

*Give the opposites of the following words:*

1 Pride
2 Attraction
3 Ingress
4 Insertion
5 Silence
6 Knowledge
7 Question
8 Health
9 Improvement
10 Safety
11 Convex
12 Innocence
13 Discord
14 Success
15 Wealth
16 Credit
17 Presence
18 Cause
19 Increase
20 Friendship

1 Who wrote the hymn 'O God our help in ages past'?
2 What is meant by 'entre nous'?
3 What is meant by 'mal de mer'?
4 Whose residence is Lambeth Palace?
5 What are the territorial divisions of U.S.A. called?
6 What was the former name of Oslo?
7 What is a caesura?
8 Who composed *Sweet and Low*?
9 In which language did the word 'Amen' originate?
10 Who was Amundsen?
11 Which famous novelist lived at Gads Hill?
12 Where is the Queen of Britain's residence in Norfolk?
13 What is an anaconda?
14 What is apiculture?
15 What is the significance of three stars on the label of a brandy bottle?
16 What are the prime numbers?
17 Which is the longer, a minim or a semibreve?
18 What are smelt?
19 When is Ash Wednesday?
20 What does the name 'Christie's' convey?

*Complete the following:*

1 As hard as —
2 As proud as —
3 As pleased as —
4 As true as —
5 As cool as —
6 As old as —
7 As blind as —
8 As cold as —
9 As steady as —
10 As sound as —
11 As ugly as —
12 As soft as —
13 As happy as —
14 As right as —
15 As dry as —
16 As bold as —
17 As obstinate as —
18 As strong as —
19 As fit as —
20 As good as —
21 As plain as —
22 As large as —
23 As merry as —
24 As safe as —

*Give the meaning of:*

1 Bon mot
2 Mot juste
3 Raconteur
4 Obiter dictum
5 Edition de Luxe
6 Lettre de cachet
7 Double entente (or entendre)
8 Nom de guerre
9 Verbatim
10 Mirabile dictu
11 Ex-libris
12 Verb. sap. (Verbum satsapienti)
13 Vox populi
14 Tête à tête
15 Soi-disant
16 Sobriquet
17 Sotto voce
18 Et seq. (et sequentes)
19 Bona fide
20 Raison d'être

1 What institution is known as the 'Old Lady of Threadneedle Street'?
2 What is a trident?
3 In which book is the character Little Nell?
4 Where is the 'ceremony of the keys' performed each night?
5 Which famous poet was blind?
6 What is Parnassus?
7 Describe a hypochondriac.
8 What is an ohm?
9 Give the family name of the Swedish Royal Family.
10 Who was Cyrano de Bergerac?
11 Who was Pocahontas?
12 What do you understand by 'desiccate'?
13 What is 'Troy-weight'?
14 What is a tumulus?
15 What was the massacre of St. Bartholomew?
16 What is a tangent?
17 The strength of the wind is referred to by sailors and others according to a scale of numbers; what is the scale called?
18 Russia is frequently referred to as the 'Soviet'. What do the term mean?
19 What variation of the Dutch language is one of the official languages of South Africa?
20 What languages are normally spoken in the different parts of Switzerland?

1 What is a nectarine?
2 What part of England is famous for its cherry orchards?
3 Where do most almonds come from?
4 What fruit, grown chiefly in India, is used in making chutney, pickles and curry?
5 Lemons, limes, and oranges are what sort of fruits?
6 What fruit is commonly called after the port from which it is exported?
7 What is a medlar?
8 What is a cantaloup?
9 Where do you find pinguins?
10 What is a pawpaw?
11 What is the correct name for a bunch of bananas?
12 What are raisins?
13 Which bitter oranges are used for making marmalade?
14 What is quince, and what is it used for?
15 What is a fruit-eating animal called?
16 Which is the odd one out, and why: William, Conference, Beurre Diel, Blenheim Orange?
17 What are guavas? From what part of the world do they come?
18 What are shaddocks?
19 What is an aubergine?
20 What is a clementine?

1 What are the rice fields called?
2 Where, in Italy, is rice grown?
3 What, and where, is The Weald?
4 Excluding continents, which are the three largest islands the world?
5 What does 'the Pampas' mean, where is it and what thriv on it?
6 Where, and what is, the Gran Chaco?
7 Where is the Jasper National Park?
8 What is a national park?
9 What is the name of the national park in southern Africa
10 Where is the Black Forest?
11 Where is Old Faithful, and what is it?
12 What name is given to the grasslands of Russia?
13 Which is the odd one out, and why: Roaring Forties, typhoon, moraine, mistral and sirocco?
14 For what are the vast plains of Alberta and Saskatchewa famous?
15 What and where is the Great Barrier Reef?
16 In which forest was an English king killed by an arrow?
17 What, and where, are the Ardennes?
18 What is grown in the Black Earth of the Ukraine and the Black Earth of Texas?
19 Which city overlooks the River St. Charles and is near a very famous plain?
20 What are (a) an isthmus and (b) a delta?

1 What is slaked lime?
2 What was the Volstead Act?
3 What is a tick?
4 Who was Izaak Walton?
5 Who painted the *Hay Wain*?
6 Who created the main character of *The Vicar of Wakefield*?
7 What is a 'white elephant'?
8 Who were the Stoics?
9 What is a fez?
10 Who invented the telescope?
11 What is a martinet?
12 Who was the famous captain of the mutiny ship *The Bounty*?
13 How many acres are there in a square mile?
14 Who wrote *The Hound of the Baskervilles*?
15 What does 'The Monument' in the City of London mark?
16 What is a sextant?
17 Who was the architect who reconstructed St. Paul's Cathedral after the Great Fire?
18 What is a visa?
19 Who was the first woman M.P. to take her seat in the Houses of Parliament?
20 Why do bees swarm?

*Each blank is a town, country or nationality. Fill in the blan*

 1 S. MacManus: *The Rocky Road to —*
 2 John Masters: *— Junction*
 3 Norman Collins: *— Belongs to Me*
 4 André Maurois: *Women of —*
 5 Lin Yutang: *The Wisdom of —*
 6 Daphne du Maurier: *— Inn*
 7 Stuart Cloete: *— Giant*
 8 Vicki Baum: *Hotel —*
 9 Louis Bromfield: *Night in —*
10 Alberto Moravia: *Woman of —*
11 Henry James: *— Square*
12 Alice Tisdale Hobart: *Oil for the Lamps of —*
13 Peter Fleming: *— Adventure*
14 Frank Swinnerton: *The Women from —*
15 Elizabeth Barrett Browning: *Sonnets from the —*
16 John Brophy: *Gentleman of —*
17 Sir Edward Gibbon: *The Decline and Fall of the — Emp*
18 Thomas Mann: *Death in —*
19 Edward Bulmer Lytton: *The Last Days of —*
20 Graham Greene: *— Rock*

1 What is meant by 'marsupial'?
2 How many humps has the dromedary?
3 In which country is the koala bear found?
4 What name do we give to the young of the otter?
5 What is the female of the fox called?
6 What is meant by 'zygodactyl'?
7 Like plants, they remain fixed, they have no eyes, legs, senses or internal organs like other animals. Yet they are animals of the sea. What are they?
8 What is the tallest animal in the world?
9 What animal is reputed to have the best memory?
0 What is the biggest bird in the world?
1 What is the largest mammal in the Antarctic regions?
2 What animal does one associate with Lapland?
3 What animal figures in the story of the foundation of Rome?
4 What animal is sacred to Hindus?
5 Name two tail-less animals.
6 What animal appears in the Old Testament story of Balaam?
7 What animal imported into Britain from North America has now become a pest?
8 What is a platypus?
9 How do sheep and cows differ in their method of grazing?
0 What is a hybrid?

1 What is 'checkmate'?
2 What is a placebo?
3 What is the Domesday Book, and who caused it to be compiled?
4 From which animal is lard obtained?
5 What is a mirage?
6 Who discovered radium?
7 What is a cassowary?
8 What is the length of the Suez Canal and when was it opened?
9 For what is the 49th parallel noted?
10 What is brass?
11 What is a palanquin?
12 Which battle laid the foundations of British rule in India?
13 What is a lac of rupees?
14 For what is Pisa noted?
15 Give the collective name for partridges.
16 What is Ellis Island?
17 Who was Sir Henry Irving?
18 What is a Magyar?
19 What do you understand by Nemesis?
20 Who was the founder of the Quakers?

1 In the Bible, who had a coat of many colours?
2 Which disciple would not believe that Jesus had risen until he had proof?
3 Members of which religion worship the Brahma?
4 What is Ramadan?
5 Who was the first to see Jesus alive on Easter Day?
6 Which day of the week is the holy day of the Muslims?
7 Members of which two religious groups refrain from eating pork?
8 Who was king of Judea at the time of Jesus' birth?
9 When did Buddha live and from which country was he?
0 What is the name for the Muslim place of worship?
1 Which day of the week is the holy day of the Jews?
2 In the Bible, where was Moses given his teaching?
3 In the Bible, what musical instrument did David play?
4 How did John the Baptist die?
5 Who was the Greek god of the sea?
6 In the story of Moses, in what terms was the Promised Land described?
7 In the Bible, how many sons did Jacob have?
8 In the Bible who was David's great friend, and whose son was he?
9 What is the Adhan?
0 What is the Bhagvad Gita?

1 What is it that sweeps clean?
2 What should be made while the sun shines?
3 'Evil . . . grow apace.'
4 According to the saying who must he pay to call the tune
5 'Tall oaks from little . . . grow.'
6 Cut your coat according to your . . .
7 What does 'under one's vine and fig tree' mean?
8 What is it that a rolling stone will not gather?
9 'Pleasures are like . . . spread.'
10 'One grain of . . . is worth a cartload of hay.'
11 'Much cry, little . . .'
12 'It's a . . . that shows the way the wind blows.'
13 What do little strokes fell?
14 Ne'er cast what till May be out?
15 In the saying, nine of these can be saved by one in time.
16 What expression is used when it is said that a son resembles his father?
17 According to the poet Charles Wolfe, what was the first thing not heard at the burial of Sir John Moore?
18 'Ruth stood breast-high amid the . . .' wrote Thomas Hood.
19 'Give me somewhere to stand and I will move . . .' said Archimedes. What would he move, and with what?
20 Which is the odd one out, and why? *A Winter's Tale*, *A Midsummer Night's Dream*, *The Last Rose of Summer*, *Twelfth Night*.

1 What is dementia?
2 What is a biretta?
3 Which famous figure in English history had a wart on his face?
4 Where and what is the ward-room?
5 What is a wadi?
6 What is a still-room?
7 Give the meaning of 'coup d'état'.
8 What is the Alhambra?
9 What is an amnesty?
10 Give a more simple name for vertigo.
11 What is a dactyl?
12 What colour is gentian?
13 What is Lloyd's Register?
14 What is a chapter house?
15 What is a cameo?
16 What is an elver?
17 At what period of the year do the Jews celebrate the Feast of the Passover?
18 Who was Karl Marx?
19 What is a lintel?
20 State the name and nationality of the author of *Hiawatha*.

1 What is the white, or bluish, precious stone from Brazil and the Urals?
2 What is nickel, and what is it used for?
3 What is another name for mercury?
4 What are the chief minerals found in granite?
5 Mix tin with antimony, bismuth or copper to get what?
6 What is nacre?
7 What is used to harden steel which is used to make cutting tools?
8 What have the red garnet and the blue sapphire in common?
9 What is natural diamond?
10 One of the main sources of atomic energy comes from Canada. What is the material?
11 In which crown is the famous ruby of the Black Prince?
12 For what is the Witwatersrand famous?
13 What is peridot?
14 Which is the alloy — copper, bronze, tin or gold?
15 What is steatite?
16 What are the jewels in a watch?
17 What is ormolu and what is it used for?
18 Which is the odd one out, and why: diamond, emerald, topaz, opal and amethyst?
19 What is alabaster?
20 What is basalt?

*What is the origin of the following:*

1 'I'll put a girdle round the earth in forty minutes.'
2 'Was this the face that launch'd a thousand ships. . .?'
3 'Out of this nettle, danger, we pluck this flower, safety.'
4 'Uneasy lies the head that wears the crown.'
5 'As good almost kill a man as kill a good book: who kills a
   man kills a reasonable creature, God's image; but he who
   destroys a good book, kills reason itself.'
6 'The play's the thing.'
7 'To see her is to love her,
   And love but her for ever.'
8 'The pen is mightier than the sword.'
9 'A ship, an isle, a sickle moon —
   With few but with how splendid stars.'
10 'It is a far, far better thing that I do, than I have ever
   done.'
11 'Stimulate the phagocytes.'
12 'The quality of mercy is not strain'd.'
13 'Nobody tells me anything.'
14 ''Twas brilig, and the slithy toves
   did gyre and gimble in the wabe,'
15 'This city now doth like a garment wear
   The beauty of the morning:'
16 'God bless us every one!'
17 'All the world's a stage.'
18 'Dost sometimes counsel take — and sometimes tea.'
19 'Oh, the cleverness of me!'
20 'Spare the rod and spoil the child.'

1 What is an affidavit?
2 Who painted the *Laughing Cavalier*?
3 What is hydrophobia?
4 Who was John D. Rockefeller?
5 What does 'dwt.' stand for?
6 What is the difference between slander and libel?
7 What does a gallon of water weigh?
8 Where is the Bois de Boulogne?
9 Give the last letter of the Greek alphabet.
10 What were the previous names of Leningrad?
11 Which is known as the Eternal City?
12 Who is the Aga Khan?
13 What is the Dail?
14 With what name is the discovery of the Law of Gravity associated?
15 What is Hobson's choice?
16 In the chanting of psalms, what are the divisions called?
17 What is a sporran?
18 Who invented the telephone?
19 What is afforestation?
20 The names of Caxton and Bodoni have a special connection with a craft. Which one?

*ach blank is a colour. What colour?*

1 C. S. Forester: — *on Resolution*
2 Edmund Spenser: *Una and the — Cross Knight*
3 Mazo de la Roche: — *oaks*
4 Stanley Weyman: *Under the — Robe*
5 John Dickson Carr: — *Spectacles*
6 John Buchan: — *mantle*
7 G. K. Chesterton: *Ballad of the — Horse*
8 H. E. Bates: *The — Plain*
9 R. L. Stevenson: *The — Arrow*
10 John Galsworthy: *The — Spoon*
11 Conan Doyle: *A Study in —*
12 Evadne Price: — *for Danger*
13 Alice Duer Miller: *The — Cliffs*
14 Edgar Allen Poe: *The — Bug*
15 Eric Linklater: *The — Opal*
16 Christianna Brand: — *for Danger*
17 William Makepeace Thackeray: — *Plush Papers*
18 Oscar Wilde: *The Picture of Dorian —*
19 Sir J.G. Frazer: *The — Bough*
20 Lesley Storm: — *Chiffon*

*Give the second lines of the following:*

1 'I remember, I remember'
2 'The curfew tolls the knell of parting day:'
3 'I wander'd lonely as a cloud'
4 'If I should die, think only this of me'
5 'Much have I travell'd in the realms of gold'
6 'At the corner of Wood Street, when daylight appears,'
7 'Drink to me only with thine eyes,'
8 'Fair Daffodils, we weep to see'
9 'Hail to thee, blithe spirit!'
10 'I am monarch of all I survey;'
11 'I met a traveller from an antique land'
12 'My heart aches, and a drowsy numbness pains'
13 'Not a drum was heard, not a funeral note,'
14 'Of all the girls that are so smart'
15 'Oh Linden, when the sun was low,'
16 'Season of mists and mellow fruitfulness'
17 'Earth has not anything to show more fair'
18 'Shall I compare thee to a summer's day?'
19 'She walks in beauty, like the night'
20 'When I consider how my light is spent'

What is a dace?
What controls the tides?
Who was Rip Van Winkle?
What are the Beefeaters?
What is the Ku Klux Klan?
What is the capital of Burma?
What is Esperanto?
Who were the Druids?
What was the Treaty of Versailles?
What is an oasis?
Who created the character Mickey Mouse?
When is American Independence Day?
Where and what are the Doldrums?
What is a fathom?
Where is Holborn?
What does the musical term 'diminuendo' mean?
Who performs the crowning ceremony at the Coronation?
Which is the second book of the Bible?
Who wrote *Ivanhoe*?
Give the meaning of 'locum tenens'.

1 In which book does the character Man Friday appear?
2 What is lava?
3 What is a larva?
4 What name is given to the end of a field where a plough turns round?
5 What is a cromlech?
6 What is a hybrid?
7 Which is the highest mountain in the world?
8 What is the Parliament or legislative assembly of Spain called?
9 What are Mormons?
10 What is Treasure Trove?
11 What is the largest mammal in the world?
12 Where was the headquarters of the League of Nations?
13 Who wrote *Pilgrim's Progress*?
14 What is a Charter Party?
15 What is buna?
16 What does 'stet' mean?
17 What is the main difference between burglary and house-breaking?
18 What is the Parliament or legislative assembly in the United States called?
19 What was the Polish corridor?
20 What is pemmican?

What are hieroglyphics?

Which famous French prison was attacked in 1789 at the beginning of the French Revolution?

Who was Methuselah? How long did he live?

Who was the author of *The Imitation of Christ*?

What is a creole?

Who was Mrs. Grundy?

What is Buridan's ass?

What do you understand of property which is entailed?

What are non-ferrous metals?

What is meant by 'lèse-majesté'?

The Quai d'Orsay in Paris was often in the news in pre-war days: what did it signify?

Describe verdigris.

The Nobel Prizes are internationally known. How did they originate and for what are they awarded?

Who was Garibaldi?

What is an aide-de-camp?

What is known as the 'granite city'?

What is an aqueduct?

Who was Father Gapon?

What is bas relief?

What was 'The New Deal'?

*Each blank represents a number. What number?*

1 Alexandre Dumas: — *Years After*
2 Charles Dickens: *A Tale of* — *Cities*
3 Vicente Blasco Ibanez: *The* — *Horsemen of the Apocalypse*
4 Agatha Christie: —, —, *Buckle My Shoe*
5 Monica Dickens: — *Pair of Feet*
6 Jules Verne: — *Weeks in a Balloon*
7 John Fletcher: *The* — *Noble Kinsmen*
8 Walter de la Mare: *The* — *Mulla Mulgars*
9 Rudyard Kipling: — *Seas*
10 H. E. Bates: — *Sisters*
11 Cecil Roberts: *Victoria* — —
12 Louisa M. Alcott: — *Cousins*
13 Charles Dana: — *Years Before the Mast*
14 Ellery Queen: — *Days Wonder*
15 John Buckan: — *Hostages*
16 Francis Beeding: — *Were Brave*
17 A. J. Cronin: — *Loves*
18 Anton Chekhov: *The* — *Sisters*
19 D. E. Stevenson: — *Graces*
20 Dennis Wheatley: — *Days to Live*

1 What is the chinook?
2 Who said 'Never in the field of human conflict was so much owed by so many to so few,' and to whom did these words refer?
3 What was the Crystal Palace?
4 What is Hansard?
5 What is meant by 'canonize'?
6 What is a centaur?
7 Who was Pliny the Younger?
8 What is an anachronism?
9 What does the word 'ANZAC' stand for?
0 What is the well known Welsh tune in the minor key sung to 'Jesus, Lover of my Soul'?
1 What is a Muscovite?
2 In which of Shakespeare's plays do these words occur: 'The quality of mercy is not strained'?
3 What is Bank rate?
4 What is the Taj Mahal?
5 What is the Zionist Movement?
6 Who wrote the words 'Unto the pure all things are pure'?
7 What is an 'escargot' on a menu?
8 What is the meaning of 'prehensile feet'?
9 What is cynosure?
0 What is a sinecure?

1 To what do the terms 'gules' and 'purpure' relate?
2 What are 'castles in Spain'?
3 What is a synod?
4 What is the Anglo-Israelite theory?
5 What is krypton?
6 Who designed the Spitfire?
7 Who was Grinling Gibbons?
8 What are Franc-tireurs?
9 Who was the British Prime Minister when war was declared in 1939?
10 What is saltpetre?
11 Who said 'If we are not governed by God we shall be r by tyrants'?
12 What is the 'Hat Trick'?
13 Who wrote *Alice in Wonderland*?
14 With what does the science of conchology deal?
15 What is a deciduous tree?
16 Give the meaning of 'sine die'.
17 Which Golf Club is known as 'The Royal and Ancient'
18 What is the spleen?
19 What is an insurance underwriter?
20 What is phrenology?

What is a dew pond?

What was the *Marie Celeste*?

Give the meaning of 'locus standi'.

Who wrote *War and Peace*?

Where is the Bodleian Library?

Who first declared war on Germany in 1939, Britain or France?

Who was Rasputin?

Who invented sandwiches?

What were the names of the Fairy King and Queen in *A Midsummer Night's Dream*?

Who was Sir Isaac Pitman?

'Inscrutable as the . . . . .'. Supply the last word.

What is an ellipse?

Printing type is measured in 'points': how many points are there in an inch?

What is (i) a metric ton, (ii) a long ton, (iii) a short ton?

What is the Pentateuch?

To what does the word 'Vulgate' refer?

What does Mgr. stand for?

Can ignorance of the law be advanced as a defence in a law action?

What is an escutcheon?

Who discovered the North Pole?

1 Who said at the New York Custom House, 'I have noth[
   to declare except my genius'?
2 In which play do the words, 'Friends, Romans,
   Countrymen,' appear?
3 Who wrote, 'All the world's a stage, and all the men an[
   women merely players'?
4 Which British Prime Minister made the statement, 'My
   lips are sealed'?
5 Which psalm has the words, 'He maketh me to lie down
   green pastures'?
6 Who said, 'England expects every man will do his duty'
7 Who called England 'A nation of shopkeepers'?
8 Where do these words appear, 'Go to the ant, thou
   sluggard. Consider her ways and be wise'?
9 Who said, 'We are not amused'?
10 Add the next five words of the quotation which starts
   'Render unto Caesar . . . . .'
11 Who refers to 'The thorn in the flesh'?
12 Who said, 'My patience is exhausted'?
13 Where do the words appear, 'No man can serve two
   masters'?
14 Who said that 'Government of the people by the people
   for the people shall not perish from the earth'?
15 Supply the missing word in the following quotation,
   'There's a . . . . . that shapes our ends, rough hew them
   how we will.'
16 When asked by a lady why he defined 'pastern' as the
   'knee' of a horse in his dictionary, who replied 'Ignoran[
   madam, pure ignorance'?
17 Who said that the Battle of Waterloo was won on the
   playing fields of Eton?
18 Who said, 'Father, I cannot tell a lie, I did it with my lit[
   hatchet'?
19 Which statesman was known for his phrase, 'Wait and
   see'?
20 Who said, 'As for me, all I know is that I know nothing'

# ANSWERS

**General Knowledge**

Esau
Superior of a community
of nuns
Wooden barrels
Grimm Bros. and Hans
Andersen
An appliance to arrest
bleeding
*Alice in Wonderland*
Stratford-on-Avon
Vixen
25th March
Another name for a
rabbit
It is the Holy City of the
Mohammedans,
containing the Shrine of
Mohammed
A small duck
Romulus and Remus
William Tell
One
St. David
Mark used for denoting
purity of gold and silver
An accomplished fact; a
deed already done
1952
A flail

**2  Sports and Occupations**

1  A lepidopterist
2  A bellringer
3  Gladiators
4  Plymouth Hoe
5  A taxidermist
6  Polo
7  A crown of laurels
8  Croquet
9  Rugby union
10  Archery
11  Eton School, England
12  Lord Rosebery
13  Jousting
14  Shakespeare in *Anthony
& Cleopatra*
15  Professional Golfers'
Association
16  Chariot racing
17  Marathon and Athens
18  A target released from a
trap in shooting
19  Standard rules for boxing
drawn up by the English
Marquess of Queensberry
20  A rodeo

### 3 Religions

1. Jacob
2. A Muslim leader of prayers
3. Saul
4. Saviour
5. Hinduism
6. The mountains of Ararat
7. An olive leaf
8. The festival at the end of Ramadan in the Muslim faith
9. St. Francis of Assissi
10. Constantine the Great
11. Tablets of stone
12. The Pope
13. Forbidden food. The opposite of kosher
14. Aaron
15. Vulcan
16. St. Catherine
17. The Qur'an or Koran
18. In the Punjab region of India
19. Synagogue
20. Medina

### 4 General Knowledge

1. A seat fixed on an elephant's back
2. Robert Raikes
3. The killing of one man by another
4. It has no tail
5. An unexplained interval
6. Cygnet
7. An instrument for indicating musical time
8. An exaggeration
9. British Broadcasting Corporation
10. A feast of the Roman church on the 2nd February
11. Ignatius Loyola
12. *Julius Caesar* (Shakespeare)
13. Fourth part of a standardised sheet of paper
14. A native tribe in South Africa
15. By virtue of office
16. The official Washington residence of the President of the United States
17. Diamond-cutting
18. Twenty-four
19. To die without leaving a Will
20. A too-often repeated phrase.

## Plant Life

Flax

A very hard wood belonging to the eucalyptus family. Found in western Australian forests

The cell walls of plants are made of it.

The main stalk bearing a solitary flower or other stalks

The raphia palm which grows mainly in Madagascar

Laurel

Maidenhair or gingko

Chlorophyll

Gramineae (The grass family)

It is the resin of certain pine trees

One which lives for more than two years

Latex

Rice paper is made from the pith of a tall shrub which grows in the swampy forests of Formosa

Nutmeg and mace

The golden wattle or acacia

The cell tissues lying between the old wood and the bark. Where annual growth takes place. Shows up as rings.

Redwood. It is soft. The others are hard woods.

It is derived from opium

Spongy bark of the cork oak tree

Eucalyptus

## 6 Threes

1 Tom, Dick and Harry
2 *Three Men in a Boat*
3 Shadrach, Meshach and Abednego
4 Wynken, Blynken and Nod
5 To Bethlehem
6 Job
7 *Three Blind Mice*
8 *Old King Cole*
9 Three little kittens
10 *Macbeth*
11 Tricorn
12 Company (Two's company; three's a crowd)
13 Trio
14 Trident
15 Trivet
16 Alexandre Dumas
17 *The Mikado*
18 The Brontë Sisters — Currer, Ellis and Acton Bell
19 Hear no evil; see no evil; speak no evil
20 Fleur-de-lys

## 7 General Knowledge

1 King Arthur's sword
2 Miguel Cervantes
3 A Jewish Festival observed 50 days after the Passover
4 System of reading and writing used by blind, consisting of raised dots on paper
5 Gander
6 Someone with a fear or hatred of cats
7 29th September
8 Departments
9 The sperm whale
10 Very loud
11 The week beginning Palm Sunday
12 A substance like rubber, but not so elastic, used mainly for insulating submarine cables
13 An Italian pioneer in wireless telegraphy
14 Mercury
15 500
16 8,000 miles
17 One-hundredth part of a metre, equivalent to .39 inches
18 A system of land tenure involving service to higher authority
19 A solid mass of metal cast in a mould
20 The central part between the west door and the choir

## 8 Minerals in Sayings

1 His money (or gold)
2 Gold
3 Coals
4 Roads
5 All level and correct
6 Stones. By those living glass houses
7 Words
8 A watched pot
9 Penny
10 Jewel
11 Coronets
12 Pen; Sword
13 Star
14 Through the eye of a needle
15 Because everything he touched turned to gold. Finally his daughter turned to gold.
16 While the iron is hot
17 Iron bars
18 His castle
19 England
20 Pirates tried to ransom Julius Caesar for 20 talents. He offered to pay 50 for his life.

## Tennis

Frank Sedgman in 1951

78 feet

1900

Every year

John McEnroe

Martina Navratilova

1977

Seven (or, if six-all is reached, a clear margin of two points)

When it forms part of a continuous stroke

The player who received serve on the first point of the tie-break

Goolagong

Jan Kodes

U.S.A.

The most Wimbledon titles held by one person (19), beaten by Billie-Jean King

Wimbledon, the US Open, the Australian Open and the French Open

Yannick Noah

Flushing Meadow, New York

Ken Rosewall

Bjorn Borg

Frew McMillan

## 10 General Knowledge

1 Charlotte Brontë

2 A skin disease

3 St. Luke

4 Person who is accepted

5 Carbon monoxide

6 An instrument for measuring the moisture in the atmosphere

7 The old Palace of the Czars in Moscow now the residence of Russian premier

8 A slaughter-house

9 Ambassadors

10 20 inches by 15 inches

11 Jenny Lind

12 Samuel Clemens

13 One hour's work done by one man. Used as means of computation in industry

14 Oliver Goldsmith

15 A homogeneous mixture of oil and water prepared by adding a third substance which combines with both, so that on shaking the oil and water do not separate

16 Fourteen

17 Woodrow Wilson

18 Gilbert and Sullivan

19 International seaplane racing

20 A plant used for salads

## 11 Pop Music

1 First long playing record by an artiste
2 The leading American weekly music newspapers
3 Britains two leading music newspapers *New Musical Express*, *Melody Maker*
4 Top of the Pops
5 American Bandstand
6 The 1950s American DJ said to have coined the expression 'rock'n'roll'
7 Electric Light Orchestra
8 The best selling pop music single records
9 Electronic keyboard
10 Jerry Lee Lewis
11 The Beatles
12 Rolling Stones
13 Buddy Holly, the Big Bopper and Ritchie Valens
14 Eddie Cochran
15 Internationally famous Swedish pop group
16 Tamla Motown — named from 'the motor city'
17 The best selling single in any week
18 Records
19 BBC's Radio 1
20 Styles of Jamaican originated black music

## 12 Cities and Ports

1 Hobart
2 Edinburgh
3 Venice
4 Moscow
5 Berne
6 Leningrad
7 Pakistan
8 Salt Lake City
9 Tananarive
10 Brasilia
11 All names for the same city. Now called Istanbul
12 Has a good stretch of water leading to it from the sea and also has four tides a day instead of the normal two.
13 The capital of Ethiopia. Country's other name is Abyssinia
14 Plymouth, Massachusetts. In 1620
15 Ostia
16 Paris, Edinburgh, New York and London
17 Birmingham. Others are regional capital towns of the British Isles
18 All are holy cities
19 Both are very important steel cities. U.S.A. and England
20 Amsterdam, Holland

84

**General Knowledge**

About
Between the ground and first floors
Henry Morton Stanley, who found the missing missionary Livingstone in Africa. A journalist
Fungus which grows underground and is used as a delicacy in cooking
Green
A disease of the bones
English portrait painter of the eighteenth century
Proof of a Will
Six
Female
An 18th century cabinet maker whose name is applied to a style of furniture of that period
Diamonds
The New Testament (Matthew 11:15)
A beginner
Continental name for stock exchange or money market
Aristocracy
Four inches
British society to preserve places of natural beauty and historic interest
The right-hand side looking forward
Yes

**14 Literature**

1 Dickens
2 Shakespeare
3 *Pickwick Papers*
4 *Vanity Fair*
5 Fairy tales
6 Louisa M. Alcott
7 John Buchan (Lord Tweedsmuir)
8 J.M. Barrie
9 A.A. Milne
10 Mathematics
11 (a) Conan Doyle (b) G.K. Chesterton
12 J.B. Priestley
13 Chaucer
14 The Brontës — Charlotte, Emily and Ann
15 Mrs Gaskell
16 American
17 James Boswell
18 Rip Van Winkle
19 Lord Byron
20 Jonathan Swift

## 15 Medical

1 Abnormal sensitivity to something which does not affect normal people
2 Loss of memory
3 A drug for the relief of pain (such as aspirin)
4 Diabetes
5 A remedy to counteract poison
6 Hardening of the arteries
7 The eye
8 Deficiency in Vitamin B
9 Food poisoning
10 Starch and sugar
11 The eye
12 Fear of confined spaces
13 Goitre
14 Through the bite of an animal suffering from rabies
15 Hypochondriac
16 A large gland situated behind the stomach
17 At the base of the brain
18 Windpipe
19 Dizziness
20 On the finger

## 16 General Knowledge

1 In the same place
2 0 degrees
3 A Malay dagger
4 Pioneer in electrical discoveries
5 The Three Wise Men guided by the star to the infant Jesus
6 Painting portraits
7 A record of goods or property
8 They were famous dia
9 Sir John Alcock and S William Whitten Brow (1919)
10 Cheese
11 Indispensable conditio
12 A person who holds a benefice; a term often applied to a vicar or rector
13 Three golden balls
14 John Milton
15 In Siberia, Russia
16 Leader of the Russian Revolution
17 Finishing stroke
18 December 28th
19 212 degrees
20 A four sided pillar

| Famous Landmarks | 18 Sports |
|---|---|
| Venice | 1 1851 |
| Pisa | 2 Boxing |
| Notre Dame | 3 Nelson Piquet |
| Eiffel Tower | 4 A fencing sword |
| Statue of Liberty | 5 Ice hockey |
| Pyramids and the Great | 6 Bruce Penhall |
| Sphinx | 7 Graham and Rodney |
| Kremlin | Marsh |
| Stonehenge | 8 Badminton |
| Forth Bridge | 9 American football |
| Arlington | 10 Jimmy Connors |
| Table Mountain | 11 Italy |
| Gibraltar | 12 Cricket |
| Clifton Suspension Bridge | 13 Ole Olsen |
| Etna | 14 New Zealand |
| The summit of Mount | 15 Six (plus One for the |
| Everest | conversion) |
| Land's End | 16 The Fastnet Race |
| Venice | 17 Squash |
| Athens | 18 Helsinki, Finland, in 1983 |
| Granada, Spain | 19 He won gold medals in |
| Paris | the 100 metres, the long |
| | jump and the $4 \times 100$ |
| | metres relay |
| | 20 Jayne Torvill and |
| | Christopher Dean |

## 19  General Knowledge

1 Ghost ship which is reputed to haunt various seas and be unable to reach port
2 The sun-dried kernel of the coconut, valued for its oil
3 An English poet and dramatist
4 A pain reliever
5 Storthing
6 A line on the side of a ship indicating the depth to which she can be loaded
7 Transpositions of initial letters, e.g. blushing crow, instead of crushing blow. After the Rev. W.A. Spooner
8 Panama and Suez
9 The ship in which the Pilgrim Fathers sailed to America
10 The Bible
11 Blue flag with a white square, flown when ships are about to sail
12 Berlin
13 A dance
14 Suicide
15 Loch Ness
16 A perfectly white animal
17 British MP whose work led to the abolition of slavery
18 An exchange of equal values
19 The award of the George Cross
20 Women who agitated for the right to vote

## 20  Cats, Dogs and Horse

1 Wild or half-domestic Australian dog
2 Bronco
3 Bay and white with patches
4 The cheetah. It can ru over 70 mph
5 About 34 miles per ho
6 Not a dog at all, but a North American rode
7 (a) a yearling male ho (b) kind of wild ass
8 Lynxes
9 A huge Newfoundlan dog
10 A small Spanish horse
11 A black or 'melanistic leopard
12 The wolf
13 A rare horse
14 A queen
15 The dog named Montmorency
16 Another name for the snow leopard
17 Feline
18 The giant panda is of t genus *Ailuropoda*
19 Saluki
20 America, from New Mexico south to Parag

## Flags and Emblems

Seven
Tanzania
Lion
Australia
Ethiopia
The Papal arms
A black bear
Switzerland
The cockerel
Elephant; eagle
The bear
Canada, New Zealand,
China and Wales
British merchant vessels
On the Mexican flag
Hammer and sickle
United States
Albania
St. George's, St.
Andrew's and St.
Patrick's
The paschal or holy lamb
West Germany

## 22 General Knowledge

1 The treacherous action by
the Japanese in the
Second World War when
they attacked the
American Navy without
declaration of War
2 The Rhine
3 King of Babylon
4 Anne Hathaway
5 A condition of equality
6 Change of front
7 George Bernard Shaw
8 Liffey
9 A gem
10 A pioneer of
Protestantism who lived
in France and Switzerland
in the sixteenth century.
Calvinism is founded on
his teaching
11 Sand
12 *Graf Spee*
13 Bubonic plague which
spread to England during
the fourteenth century
14 The Sunday 50 days
before Easter
15 The union of a number of
interests
16 Beethoven
17 A mark (٨) to indicate
the omission of a letter or
word
18 A breed of laying duck
19 William Shakespeare
20 Promotor of the idea of
daylight saving

## 23 Characters

1 Jonathan Swift
2 C.S. Forester
3 Hugh Lofting
4 Margaret Mitchell
5 G.B. Shaw
6 John Galsworthy
7 Joseph Addison
8 John Bunyan
9 Emily Brontë
10 Mary Wolstonecraft Shelley
11 Richard Brinsley Sheridan
12 Hugh Walpole
13 Mark Twain
14 Charles Dickens
15 William Makepeace Thackeray
16 A.A. Milne
17 Alexandre Dumas, Jnr.
18 John Buchan
19 Louisa M. Alcott
20 William Shakespeare

## 24 Golf

1 Five minutes
2 43 inches
3 Every other year
4 4½ inches
5 Only if there is a threat lightning
6 Greg Norman
7 Jack Nicklaus
8 Bernhard Langer
9 2 under par for the hol
10 2 up with 2 to play
11 1979
12 Prestwick, Scotland
13 Augusta, Georgia
14 14
15 St. Andrews, Scotland
16 Severiano Ballesteros
17 Craig Stadler
18 A golfer who can play course to par
19 5-iron
20 The amateurs of Great Britain and the U.S.A.

| General Knowledge | 26 Links |
|---|---|
| Indian religious community | 1 Shares |
| The housekeeper of a building in France | 2 Parcel |
| A hater of mankind | 3 Span |
| Winter sports | 4 Mortar |
| Naval adventurer of the 18th century who became a Commodore of the United States Navy during the War of Independence | 5 Pans |
| | 6 Nail |
| | 7 Treacle |
| | 8 Sound |
| | 9 Bit |
| | 10 Joan |
| Errors and Omissions Excepted | 11 Socket |
| Revised Version of the Bible | 12 Furbelows |
| A spout from a roof gutter in the form of a human or other figure | 13 Chattels |
| | 14 Baggage |
| | 15 Corner |
| A Russian measure of length, about 3,500 feet 1,500 miles | 16 Ruin (or Pinion) |
| | 17 Ashes |
| The time taken by the moon to complete its orbit round the earth, about 29½ days | 18 Cry |
| | 19 Means |
| | 20 Bees |

The great Chinese sage and philosopher who founded an ethical system

A place where mineral waters rise

7 a.m. Greenwich mean time

Great, swell, choir, solo

An instrument for determining the specific gravity of liquids

A Flemish portrait painter of the seventeenth century

A photograph or drawing which gradually shades away towards the edges

A shellfish

Jack Johnson

## 27 Geography

1 Helsinki
2 Off the most southern point of South America
3 U.S.A.
4 Northern Ireland
5 Goodwins
6 Isle of Anglesey
7 Ben Nevis
8 Bay of Biscay
9 Off the east coast of Africa. The Malagasy Republic
10 North-west Africa
11 Eire
12 East
13 China
14 The Sea of Marmora with the Black Sea
15 Lake Ontario
16 Victoria
17 Argentina
18 California
19 The Mediterranean and the Red Sea
20 Switzerland and Italy

## 28 General Knowledge

1 Representation of a ho overflowing with the earth's produce
2 Chicago
3 A kind of axe with a broad blade and a long handle
4 The goddess of Art
5 Hymn of thanksgiving
6 Talismans
7 The 200th anniversary
8 Jezebel
9 The seed of the flax pla
10 Johann Strauss
11 New Zealand doctor w was a pioneer in infant welfare and diet
12 (i) upper case, (ii) lowe case
13 A type of sponge consisting of the netwo of fibres in the fruit of a climbing plant
14 The supreme council of England in Anglo-Saxc times
15 Coal tar
16 A defect of the eye
17 4 p.m. to 6 p.m. (first); 6 p.m. to 8 p.m. (secon
18 The study of coins
19 Doctor of Philosophy
20 One who has entered in a contract with a professional man for a period of service with a view to qualifying in the profession

**Buildings**

The Mansion House
New York City
Wiltshire in southern England
Windsor Castle
The Statue of Liberty
The House of Lords
In front of St. Peter's, Rome
Babylon. Nebuchadnezzar
Russia
The pyramids
The Great Pyramid of Cheops
Pharos
Arromanches, Normandy in the Second World War
A circular building in Rome. A temple dedicated to all the gods
Caaba
Assisi, Italy. Paintings of the life of St. Francis
The Plain of Shinar
Rhodes
The obelisk (Cleopatra's Needle) originally taken from Heliopolis, Egypt to England. The second obelisk taken to New York Central Park
City of Granada, Spain. Ancient Moorish palace and fortress

**30 Literary Miscellany**

1 *Pilgrim's Progress*. John Bunyan
2 *The Ballad of Reading Gaol*. Oscar Wilde
3 Rugby
4 Alice
5 London and Paris. Charles Dickens
6 Meg, Jo, Beth and Amy March
7 Elia
8 Lilliput, Gargantua and Brobdignag
9 Sir Thomas More
10 Samuel Butler
11 Missolonghi in Greece
12 Shakespeare by Ben Jonson. *To the Memory of Shakespeare*
13 W.E. Gladstone by Benjamin Disraeli
14 Shakespeare by Ben Jonson. *Discoveries*
15 Hilaire Belloc. *On His Books*
16 Montmorency
17 Portia
18 Mr. Toad of Toad Hall
19 Sebastian
20 *The Scarlet Pimpernel*, Sir Percy Blakeney

## 31 General Knowledge

1 The Duke of Wellington
2 Fruit and vegetable market and the opera
3 South American of the early nineteenth century who led the movement to establish the independence of Spain's South American Colonies. Bolivia is named after him.
4 Duck
5 1866
6 A French law dating back to the sixth century, which precluded women from becoming rulers
7 Small reptile that changes colour to match its immediate background
8 Nero
9 A mistake or error of behaviour
10 Joan of Arc
11 A large flat fish
12 Group of chalk rocks off the western end of the Isle of Wight, England
13 W.M. Thackeray
14 One who dabbles in many things and specialises in none
15 Cambridge
16 A card game
17 Coventry
18 Baroness Orczy
19 Large ox found in Central Asia
20 A large root like a potato grown in the tropics

## 32 Foreign Phrases

1 To infinity
2 According to value
3 According to custom o fashion
4 To the point
5 Well acquainted with
6 A black beast; a bugbe
7 In good faith; in reality
8 As it should be
9 A stroke of policy; a violent measure in pub affairs
10 A finishing stroke
11 Too much or too many
12 In a body
13 On the way
14 Between ourselves
15 An error
16 Out of condition to figh
17 Let alone; suffer to hav its own way
18 Under consideration
19 Opposite; facing
20 Where are you going?

## 3 Food & Drink

1 A kind of shellfish
2 Whisky
3 Vodka
4 A cooked sausage between two halves of a bread roll
5 One is a free choice of the menu and the other a set meal
6 Calf
7 Sheep's milk — although some cow's and goat's milk may be added
8 Shellfish popular in North America
9 Savoury biscuits served with cocktails
10 Curly-leaved chicory, used as salad
11 Goose liver
12 By lifting it up in the fingers
13 The swift of China and India
14 An alcoholic drink taken before meals to stimulate the appetite
15 A unit of energy
16 Proteins
17 Lloyd's of London
18 Vodka and tomato juice
19 The yolk
20 Garlic

## 34 General Knowledge

1 *A Christmas Carol* by Charles Dickens
2 The Thames, known as the Isis at this point
3 About ⅕ oxygen and ⅘ nitrogen, with small quantities of other gases
4 A man who works on the construction or repair of high buildings
5 The place in the foremast of a ship, in which a look-out man is stationed
6 Paper dyed with litmus (a purple dye obtained from certain lichens) which indicates acidity or alkalinity in chemical testing by changing colour
7 Forty-two
8 Violet, indigo, blue, green, yellow, orange and red
9 Offspring of Caucasian and Negro
10 George Washington
11 Tchaikovsky
12 Moses
13 Gold, frankincense and myrrh
14 Melita, or Malta as it is now called
15 Orange, green and purple
16 Afternoon
17 Great Britain
18 Carbonate of lime hanging like an icicle from the roof of a cave
19 Abbreviated way of writing 'and' — &
20 Adolf Hitler

## 35  Husband & Wife
 1 Josephine
 2 Princess Mary of England
 3 Mrs. Simpson
 4 Elizabeth Barrett
 5 The Dauphin
 6 Marie Antoinette
 7 Ann Hathaway
 8 Boaz
 9 Leah and Rachel
10 Katharine of Aragon
11 Prince Albert
12 Princess Pocahontas
13 Mr. Knightley
14 Desdemona
15 Arthur
16 Lot's
17 Mr. Beaton's
18 Mr. and Mrs. Squeers
19 William Shakespeare
   (*Twelfth Night*)
20 Spencer

## 36  Links
 1 Sullivan
 2 *Unicorn*
 3 *The Carpenter*
 4 Horsa
 5 Cleopatra
 6 Modern
 7 Remus
 8 Gomorrah
 9 Magog
10 *Son*
11 Adonis
12 Delilah
13 Tweedledee
14 Gretel
15 Persians
16 Mary
17 Hardy
18 Hammerstein
19 Fred Astaire
20 Hutch

## General Knowledge

Priam, King of Troy
Cantons
A state ruled by the Pope;
also the palace in which
he lives
100 fathoms, i.e. 600 ft
The shaven crown of a
priest
It rises
A priest
Psalms
Peter Pan, by Sir James
Barrie
A hop-drying kiln
After Sir Robert Peel,
who made valuable Police
reforms whilst Home
Secretary
A reed from which the
ancient Egyptians made
paper
Beethoven
Siam
'I Serve'; the motto of
every Prince of Wales
Amy Johnson
Constantinople
Metal containing 22 parts
pure gold
Six
Samuel Johnson

## 38 Literary Flora

1 Mazo de la Roche
2 J.B. Priestley
3 R.C. Sherriff
4 Thomas Hardy
5 Emlyn Williams
6 Kate O'Brien
7 W. Somerset Maugham
8 John Steinbeck
9 Anton Chekov
10 Robert Bolt
11 Kenneth Grahame
12 Louis Golding
13 Paul Gallico
14 G.B. Shaw
15 Louis Bromfield
16 Margery Sharp
17 H.E. Bates
18 James Barrie
19 Sheila Kaye-Smith
20 Alexander Dumas

## 39 Missing Words

1 ship (Longfellow)
2 spot (Shakespeare — *Macbeth*)
3 swine (St. Matthew's Gospel)
4 coals (Proverbs)
5 Bird (Shelley)
6 policeman (W.S. Gilbert)
7 err (Pope)
8 thing (Keats)
9 powers (Wordsworth)
10 folly (Gray)
11 arrow (Longfellow)
12 corn (Genesis)
13 sealing wax (Lewis Carroll)
14 systems (Tennyson)
15 stands (Milton)
16 tumult (Kipling)
17 horse (Shakespeare — *Richard III*)
18 swift (Proverbs)
19 cat (Lewis Carroll)
20 mercy (Shakespeare — *Merchant of Venice*)

## 40 General Knowledge

1 Acorn
2 A Welsh arts conventio where prizes are award
3 From the root of a herbaceous plant which grows in South Europe
4 The title by which an unmarried woman is designated
5 The sap of a tropical tre
6 98.4 degrees Fahrenhe
7 1815
8 A rodent which freque northern countries
9 Approximately 39⅓ inches
10 Marshal of the Royal A Force
11 (Christian names) Cantuar
12 Tit for tat; an equivaler
13 George Gershwin
14 Cape Town, South Afr
15 Union of Socialist Sovi Republics
16 Beetle
17 A man on whom no reliance can be placed
18 A novice, a raw hand
19 Nelson's
20 The substance which be gather from flowers to make honey

**Animals in Literature**
The Cheshire Cat, in
*Alice in Wonderland*, by
Lewis Carroll
White Fang (novel by
Jack London)
Rikki Tikki Tavi, in *Kim*
*The Ancient Mariner*
Moby Dick, in that novel
by Herman Melville
Modestine, in *Travels*
*with a Donkey*, by Robert
Louis Stevenson
*Alice Through the*
*Looking-Glass* by Lewis
Carroll
The Owl and the Pussy
Cat (the poem by Edward
Lear)
A mouse, in *To a Mouse*,
by Robert Burns
Selima, in the poem by
Thomas Gray
Nana, in *Peter Pan*, by
J.M. Barrie
Black Beauty
Little Grey Rabbit, in the
books by Alison Uttley
The White Rabbit, in
*Alice in Wonderland*
Kenneth Grahame, in
*The Wind in the Willows*
The Dormouse, in *Alice*
*in Wonderland*
Long John Silver, in
*Treasure Island*, by
Robert Louis Stevenson
Rev. R.H. Bahram, in
*The Jackdaw of Rheims*
*The Pied Piper of*
*Hamelin*, by Robert
Browning
A horse, in *The Arab's*
*Farewell to his Steed*

**42 Opposites**
1 Humility
2 Repulsion
3 Egress
4 Extraction
5 Noise
6 Ignorance
7 Answer
8 Disease
9 Deterioration
10 Danger
11 Concave
12 Guilt
13 Harmony
14 Failure
15 Poverty
16 Debit
17 Absence
18 Effect
19 Decrease
20 Enmity

## 43 General Knowledge

1 Isaac Watts
2 Between ourselves
3 Sea sickness
4 The Archbishop of Canterbury
5 States
6 Christiana
7 A cut or natural pause in a line of poetry
8 Tennyson
9 Hebrew. It means 'truly', 'yes', or 'so be it'
10 Norwegian explorer. First to reach the South Pole in 1911
11 Charles Dickens
12 Sandringham
13 The largest snake on the American continent
14 Bee-keeping
15 This indicates that the contents are five years old
16 Those that are indivisible
17 Semibreve
18 Small fish
19 The first day of Lent
20 The famous London auction rooms

## 44 Proverbial Similes

1 nails
2 a peacock
3 punch
4 steel
5 a cucumber
6 the hills
7 a bat
8 charity
9 a rock
10 a bell
11 sin
12 silk
13 a sandboy
14 rain
15 dust
16 brass
17 a mule
18 a horse
19 a fiddle
20 gold
21 a pikestaff
22 life
23 a cricket
24 houses

**Foreign Words and Phrases**

A witty saying
Exactly the right word
Story-teller
Something said incidentally
A splendid edition of a book
A sealed letter (Royal warrant for arrest)
Ambiguity
Assumed name
Word for word
Wonderful to relate
From the books [of] (hence its use on book-plates)
A word is enough for a wise man
The voice of the people — public opinion
Conversation between two people
So-called
Nickname
Below the voice — an aside
And those that follow
In good faith
Reason for existence

**46 General Knowledge**

1 The Bank of England
2 A three-pronged sceptre represented in the hand of Neptune
3 *The Old Curiosity Shop* (Charles Dickens)
4 Tower of London
5 Milton
6 Mountain which figures in Greek mythology
7 One who imagines he is suffering from disease
8 A unit of electrical resistance
9 Bernadotte
10 17th century French author who fought many duels because of references to his long nose
11 Daughter of a 17th century Red Indian Chief, who saved the life of an English prisoner and married an Englishman
12 To dry out
13 System of weight measurement for gold and silver
14 Mound of earth over a burial place
15 Massacre of Protestants in Paris on St. Bartholomew's Day in 1572
16 A straight line touching an arc of a circle
17 Beaufort Scale
18 'Soviet' is Russian for workers' council
19 Africaans, otherwise Cape Dutch
20 French, German, Italian, Romansch

## 47 Fruit

1 A fruit very much like the peach, but with a smooth and waxy skin
2 Kent
3 Italy, Spain and California
4 Mango
5 Citrus fruits
6 Jaffa oranges
7 A tree with fruit like a small brown apple. It is eaten when decayed
8 A kind of melon
9 In the West Indies. It is a type of pineapple
10 It is the fruit of an American tree. The juice can be used to tenderise meat
11 Hand
12 Partially dried grapes
13 Seville
14 A hard and acid pear-shaped fruit, yellowish in colour. Used as a preserve or flavouring
15 A frugivore
16 Blenheim Orange. It is an apple and the others are varieties of pears
17 Pear-shaped fruit with sweet yellow or red pulp and kidney-shaped seeds. Grown in the West Indies
18 Large fruits from an orange-like tree. The fruit grows to as much as 15 lbs. in weight
18 The purple fruit of the egg-plant is known as an aubergine
20 A small orange citrus fruit

## 48 Geography

1 Paddy fields
2 In the central plain of t River Po
3 A forest in S.E. Englan
4 Borneo, Greenland an New Guinea
5 The plains. In Argentir Cattle
6 A vast area of forest an grassland in Paraguay
7 In the Rockies on the Western border of Alberta
8 Areas of beauty, often stocked with animals, protected by the government
9 The Kruger National Park, Transvaal
10 Germany
11 Yellowstone National Park, U.S.A. A geyser
12 The Steppes
13 Moraine is debris left after a glacier melts. Th rest are winds
14 Wheat provinces of Canada
15 A 1,200 mile coral reef the Queensland coast
16 The New Forest, Hampshire
17 A large area of forest i Belgium and extending into France and Luxembourg. Much st wild
18 Wheat. Cotton
19 Quebec on the Heights Abraham
20 (a) A narrow neck of la (b) Land enclosed by river branches

## General Knowledge

Quicklime to which water has been added

An Act passed in U.S.A. in 1919 prohibiting the sale of liquor containing more than 0.5% alcohol. 'Prohibition'

A blood-sucking parasite

Author of *The Compleat Angler*

Constable

Oliver Goldsmith

Useless possession

Followers of the Athenian philosopher, Zeno: indifferent to pleasure or pain

Male headgear worn in Mohammedan countries

Galileo

A strict disciplinarian William Bligh

640

Sir Arthur Conan Doyle

Where the Great Fire of London started

The sixth part of a circle; a navigating instrument

Sir Christopher Wren

Permission granted by a State to enter or cross its territory

Lady Astor

Because a new queen is hatched and the old one goes off with her followers

## 50  Places in Titles

1  Dublin
2  Bhowani
3  London
4  Paris
5  China
6  Jamaica
7  African
8  Berlin
9  Bombay
10  Rome
11  Washington
12  China
13  Brazilian
14  Sicily
15  Portuguese
16  Stratford
17  Roman
18  Venice
19  Pompeii
20  Brighton

## 51 Animals

1 Animal which carries its young, born imperfect, in a pouch, e.g. kangaroo
2 The dromedary has one hump
3 Australia
4 Kittens
5 Vixen
6 Having two toes pointing forward and two back as, for example, in the woodpeckers
7 Sponges
8 Giraffe
9 Elephant
10 Ostrich
11 Whale
12 Reindeer
13 Wolf
14 White cow
15 Manx cat and guinea pig
16 Ass
17 Grey squirrel
18 An aquatic mammal with dark-brown fur, webbed feet and a duck's bill. Native of Australia
19 Sheep bite with the teeth of the upper jaw, cows wrap their tongues around the grass and pull it
20 Offspring of the union of two different species

## 52 General Knowledge

1 The winning position the game of chess
2 A medicine given to please the patient rath than to effect a cure
3 A detailed survey of t land of England draw by order of William th Conqueror
4 Pig
5 An optical illusion common in the desert
6 Madame Curie
7 A bird
8 100 miles. 1869
9 The undefended boundary between Canada and U.S.A.
10 An alloy of copper an zinc
11 A covered carriage carried on the shoulde used in the East
12 Plassey, 1757
13 100,000
14 Leaning Tower
15 Covey
16 An island lying off Ne York harbour where immigrants into U.S.A are examined
17 Famous actor
18 A native of Hungary
19 Retribution
20 George Fox

## 53 Religions

1 Joseph
2 Thomas (hence 'doubting Thomas')
3 Hindus
4 A month in the Muslim calendar when fasting is required from dawn to sunset
5 Mary Magdelene
6 Friday
7 Jews and Muslims
8 Herod
9 From c. 563–483 BC. Nepal
10 The Mosque
11 Saturday
12 Mount Sinai
13 The harp
14 He was beheaded
15 Poseidon
16 As a land flowing with milk and honey
17 Twelve
18 Jonathon. Saul's son
19 The Muslim call to prayer
20 A poem of about 700 verses central to Hindu philosophy

## 54 Sayings and Titles

1 A new broom
2 Hay
3 Weeds
4 Piper
5 Acorns
6 Cloth
7 To be safe at home
8 Moss
9 Poppies
10 Pepper
11 Wool
12 Straw
13 Great oaks
14 Clout
15 Stitch
16 A chip off the old block
17 'Not a drum was heard . . .'
18 Corn
19 The Earth. A lever, for he was explaining its principles
20 *Last Rose of Summer* is a poem. All the others are plays. Written by Shakespeare

## 55 General Knowledge

1 A weakening of the intellect
2 A priest's square cap
3 Oliver Cromwell
4 On a warship; the mess room of commissioned officers
5 A dried up watercourse in arid areas
6 A service room in an hotel or restaurant
7 A sudden stroke of State policy
8 Moorish palace at Granada, Spain
9 A general pardon for offenders
10 Giddiness
11 A long syllable followed by two short ones
12 Blue
13 A list of vessels classified according to seaworthiness and published by Lloyd's Register of Shipping
14 A meeting place for clergy
15 A carved gem on which figures are cut in relief
16 A young eel
17 Easter
18 German Socialist who expounded a complete theory and scheme for the Socialist Order
19 Horizontal stone or beam over a door or window
20 Henry Wadsworth Longfellow, an American

## 56 Precious Stones

1 Beryl
2 A silvery metal, hard and magnetic. Small amounts are used to harden and strengthen steel
3 Quicksilver
4 Quartz, feldspar and mic
5 Pewter
6 The lining of the oyster shell; mother-of-pearl
7 Molybdenum
8 The garnet and sapphire are both transparent
9 Fused carbon
10 Uranium
11 The Imperial Crown of State
12 Its gold mines
13 Olivine, a green gem
14 Bronze
15 Soapstone. A kind of tale
16 They vary, but the most common is a synthetic ruby material
17 Gilded bronze. Used for decorating furniture
18 Opal. The others are transparent but opal is ne
19 A name given to the several varieties of carbonate or sulphate of lime
20 Brown or dark green volcanic rock

1 William Shakespeare: *A Midsummer Night's Dream* (Puck)

2 Christopher Marlow: *Doctor Faustus* (of Helen)

3 Shakespeare: *Henry IV, Part I* (Hotspur)

4 Shakespeare: *Henry IV, Part II* (King Henry)

5 John Milton: *Areopagitica*

6 Shakespeare: *Hamlet*

7 Robert Burns: *Bonnie Lesley*

8 Edward Bulwyer Lytton: *Richelieu*

9 James Elroy Flecker (the poem of that name)

10 Charles Dickens: *A Tale of Two Cities* (Sidney Carton)

11 G.B. Shaw: *The Doctor's Dilemma* (Ralph Bloomfield Bonington 'BB')

12 Shakespeare: *The Merchant of Venice* (Portia)

13 John Galsworthy: *Man of Property* (James Forsyte)

14 Lewis Carrol: *Alice through the Looking Glass*

15 William Wordsworth: *Upon Westminster Bridge*

16 Charles Dickens: *A Christmas Carol* (Tiny Tim)

17 Shakespeare: *As You Like It* (Jacques)

18 Alexander Pope: *The Rape of the Lock*

19 J.M. Barrie: *Peter Pan*

20 Samuel Butler: *Hudibras*

1 A written statement of facts made upon oath

2 Franz Hals

3 A disease communicated by a bite from a rabid animal, also known as rabies

4 American oil magnate

5 Pennyweight

6 Slander is spoken; libel is written or recorded in some other manner

7 Ten pounds

8 On the outskirts of Paris

9 Omega

10 St. Petersburg and Petrograd

11 Rome

12 Indian Potentate, the head of the Ismaeli Mohammedans

13 Irish Parliament

14 Sir Isaac Newton

15 None — Take what is offered

16 Pointing

17 A pouch worn in front of a Highlander's kilt

18 Graham Bell

19 The planting of trees to provide the forests of the future

20 Printing

## 59 Literary Colours

1 Brown
2 Red
3 White
4 Red
5 Black
6 Green
7 White
8 Purple
9 Black
10 Silver
11 Scarlet
12 Red
13 White
14 Gold
15 Black
16 Green
17 Yellow
18 Gray
19 Golden
20 Black

## 60 First Lines

1 'The house where I was born,'
2 'The lowing herd wind slowly o'er the lea;'
3 'That floats on high o'er vales and hills,'
4 'That there's some corner of a foreign field'
5 'And many goodly states and kingdoms seen;'
6 'Hangs a Thrush that sings loud, it has sung for three years:'
7 'And I will pledge with mine;'
8 'You haste away so soon'
9 'Bird thou never wert,'
10 'My right there is none to dispute;'
11 'Who said: Two vast and trunkless legs of stone'
12 'My sense, as though of hemlock I had drunk,'
13 'As his corpse to the rampart we hurried;'
14 'There's none like pretty Sally;'
15 'All bloodless lay the untrodden snow;'
16 'Close bosom-friend of the maturing sun;'
17 'Dull would he be of soul who could pass by'
18 'Thou art more lovely and more temperate:'
19 'Of cloudless climes and starry skies.'
20 'Ere half my days, in this dark world and wide,'

## General Knowledge

1 A fresh water fish
2 The moon
3 The character, who fell asleep for twenty years, created by Washington Irving in a short story
4 Yeomen of the Guard (of the Tower of London)
5 A secret association founded in the Southern States of America with racist objects
6 Rangoon
7 International language invented by Dr. Zamenhof
8 Priests of ancient Britain
9 The conditions of peace imposed in 1919 after the First World War
10 Fertile area in the desert due to the presence of water
11 Walt Disney
12 4th July
13 Areas of almost windless calm ocean near the Equator
14 Six feet
15 In London
16 Gradually softer
17 The Archbishop of Canterbury
18 Exodus
19 Sir Walter Scott
20 One acting temporarily for another

**General Knowledge**

1 *Robinson Crusoe*
2 The molten substance erupted from a volcano
3 An insect grub
4 Headland
5 A large flat stone laid horizontally on upright ones
6 A cross breed
7 Everest, in the Himalayas. 29,141 feet
8 Cortes
9 Religious sect in America who sanctioned polygamy
10 Gold or silver found hidden, the owner being unknown
11 Blue whale
12 Geneva, Switzerland
13 John Bunyan
14 A contract for the hire of a ship for the conveyance of goods
15 Artificial rubber
16 Let it stand
17 Burglary is committed at night and house-breaking in the daytime
18 Congress
19 A strip of territory formerly German, awarded to Poland after the First World War, to give her access to the sea
20 Lean meat, dried and pressed into cakes; a food for long voyages

### 63 General Knowledge

1 Writing in pictures used by the Egyptians
2 The Bastille
3 Grandfather of Noah; he lived for 969 years
4 Thomas à Kempis
5 One of European descent born in S. America or the W. Indies
6 A character epitomising all that is proper
7 Indecisive man: from a sophism by Buridan
8 Property which descends to heirs who may use it but not dispose of it
9 Metals containing no iron
10 High treason
11 The French Foreign Office, which was there
12 The bluish-green rust on copper, brass or bronze after prolonged exposure
13 Annual awards instituted by Alfred Nobel, the Swedish chemist, for the greatest contributions to learning and peace
14 An Italian soldier and patriot (1807–1882) important in the foundation of modern Italy
15 Officer serving in a confidential capacity
16 Aberdeen
17 A bridge carrying water
18 A Russian revolutionary who led the strikes in St. Petersburg in the early 20th century
19 Sculpture partially raised from a background
20 President Roosevelt's scheme to overcome the 1930s' slump in the USA

### 64 Numbers in Titles

1 Twenty
2 Two
3 Four
4 One, two
5 One
6 Five
7 Two
8 Three
9 Seven
10 Two
11 4.30
12 Eight
13 Two
14 Ten
15 Three
16 Eleven
17 Three
18 Three
19 Four
20 Sixty

**General Knowledge**

Warm dry wind in the E. Rockies, 55°–60°N.

Winston Churchill, 1940. To the fighter pilots who drove back the German planes during The Battle of Britain

Great public building mainly of glass and iron. Originally in Hyde Park it was moved to Sydenham 1854, and burnt down 1936

The official record of Parliamentary proceedings.

To declare a saint

A mythological figure, half man, half horse

Roman figure famous for his letters

Assignment of events or persons to a period outside that to which they belong

Australian and New Zealand Army Corps

Aberystwyth

A native of Moscow

*The Merchant of Venice* (Portia)

The rate of interest on Bank loans fixed by the Bank of England

Mausoleum of great splendour at Agra, India

Movement to re-establish the Jews in Palestine

St. Paul in his letter to Titus (1:15)

An edible snail

Feet which are capable of seizing and holding

Centre of attraction

A paid position with little work attached

1 Colours in heraldry (red and purple)
2 Imaginary schemes or plans
3 A council of religious people
4 That the British race is descended from the ten lost tribes of Israel
5 A rare gas present in the air
6 R.J. Mitchell
7 Famous woodcarver
8 Irregular troops
9 Neville Chamberlain
10 Popular name for potassium nitrate: constituent of gunpowder
11 William Penn
12 Three consecutive successes
13 Lewis Carroll
14 Shells
15 One whose leaves fall in the autumn
16 No date fixed
17 St. Andrew's
18 An organ of the body which enriches the blood
19 One who sets his name to an insurance policy and becomes answerable for loss or damage in return for payment of a certain premium
20 A system which professes to define a person's ability and character from the shape of the head

## 67 General Knowledge

1 A pond which forms on high ground and insulated underneath so that the dew collects and does not evaporate
2 A sailing ship which was found deserted on the high seas with everything in order but no life on board
3 Ground to stand on: an acknowledged right
4 Tolstoy
5 Oxford
6 Britain
7 A sinister Russian monk with strong power over the Russian Royal Family
8 The Earl of Sandwich. When playing cards he would not eat a proper meal, and so placed meat between pieces of bread and ate it at the card table
9 Oberon and Titania
10 Inventor of the famous shorthand system
11 Sphinx
12 A regular oval
13 72
14 (i) 2,204 lb., (ii) 2,240 lb., (iii) 2,000 lb.
15 A name for the first five books of the Bible
16 4th century Latin Bible
17 Monsignor — a Roman Catholic title
18 No
19 A family shield on which a Coat of Arms has been emblazoned
20 Robert Peary

## 68 Quotations

1 Oscar Wilde
2 *Julius Caesar*
3 Shakespeare
4 Rt. Hon. Stanley Baldwin
5 Twenty-third Psalm
6 Lord Nelson
7 Napoleon
8 Book of Proverbs
9 Queen Victoria
10 'the things that are Caesar's.'
11 St. Paul
12 Hitler
13 The Sermon on the Mount
14 Abraham Lincoln
15 'divinity' (*Hamlet*, Shakespeare)
16 Samuel Johnson
17 The Duke of Wellington
18 George Washington
19 Lord Asquith
20 Socrates